JONAH
An Old Testament Story
BEVERLY BRODSKY

J. B. LIPPINCOTT COMPANY
Philadelphia and New York

**For Mildred Newman Berkowitz,
a special friend**

U.S. Library of Congress Cataloging in Publication Data.   Brodsky, Beverly.   Jonah:
an Old Testament story.   SUMMARY: Jonah relates his experiences when he disobeyed
God's command.   1. Jonah, the prophet. 2. Prophets—Biography. 3. Bible. O.T.—
Biography. [1. Jonah, the prophet. 2. Bible stories—O.T.] I. Title.   BS580.J55B7
224'.92'0924 [B]   77-5925   ISBN-0-397-31733-6

I am Jonah, son of Amittai
and a servant of the Lord.
My people call me a prophet,
for they believe that
I am filled with
the wisdom of the Lord.

One day I heard God call my name. "Jonah," he commanded, "go to Nineveh and tell its people that they have sinned. Warn them that I will destroy their city and everything that lives there."

It is true that I am a Hebrew and that I fear the Lord God of heaven who made the sea and dry land, but I did not obey him. The people of Nineveh worship other gods. What does my god have to do with them?

I fled to Joppa, where I
found a ship that would take
me to Tarshish.

I felt free, as though a great burden had been lifted
from me. I went below deck and soon fell fast asleep.

I awakened to a nightmare. We were far out at sea
and the ship was caught in a storm.

Lightning struck all around us and gales of wind tore the masts from the deck. The ship groaned as though it would break in two.

"Pray to your gods for mercy!" the captain cried out. "A great god is angry!"

"I am to blame," I said. "I thought I could run away from God, but he has followed me. You must throw me overboard or we will all perish."

Though they knew I spoke the truth, the men tried desperately to bring the ship to dry land. But it was no use. The storm only grew worse, and they threw me into the raging sea.

The storm ended
and a giant fish
swallowed me up.

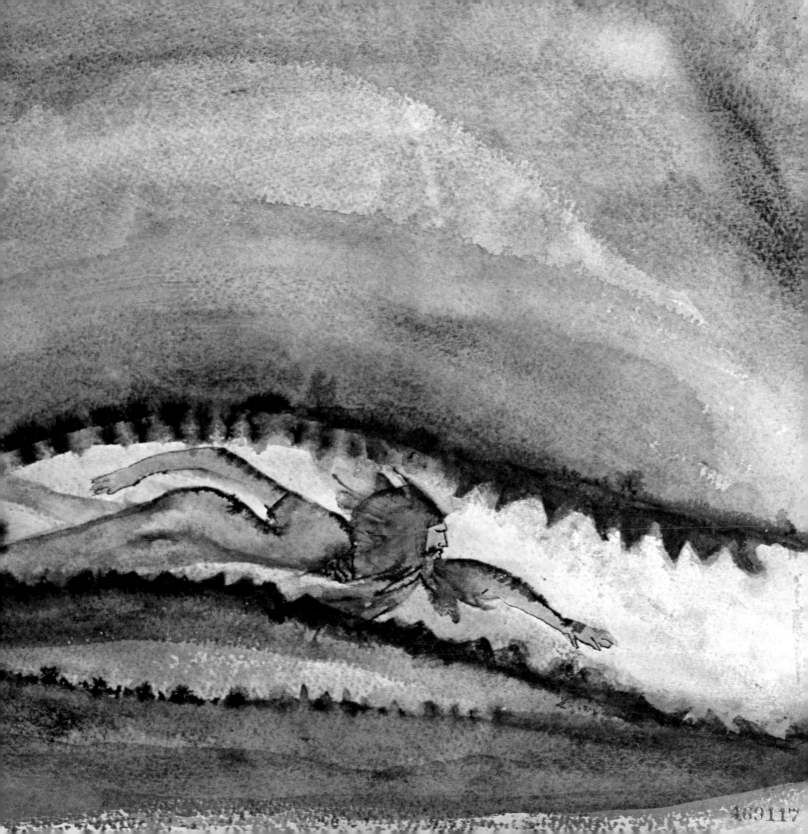

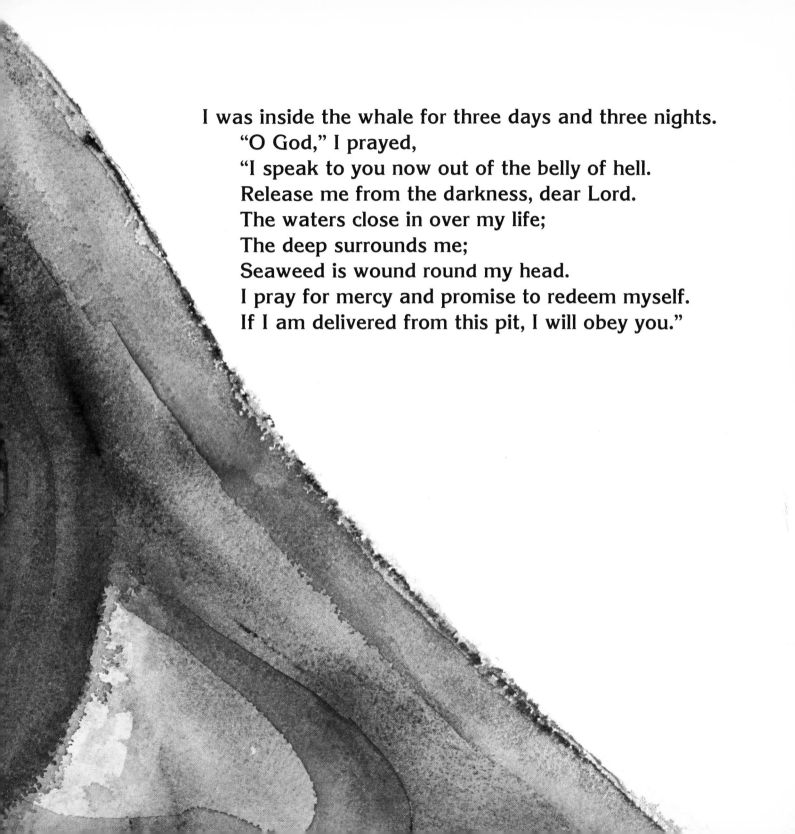

I was inside the whale for three days and three nights.
   "O God," I prayed,
   "I speak to you now out of the belly of hell.
   Release me from the darkness, dear Lord.
   The waters close in over my life;
   The deep surrounds me;
   Seaweed is wound round my head.
   I pray for mercy and promise to redeem myself.
   If I am delivered from this pit, I will obey you."

When the Lord God heard this,
he spoke to Leviathan
and the giant beast delivered me
to dry land.

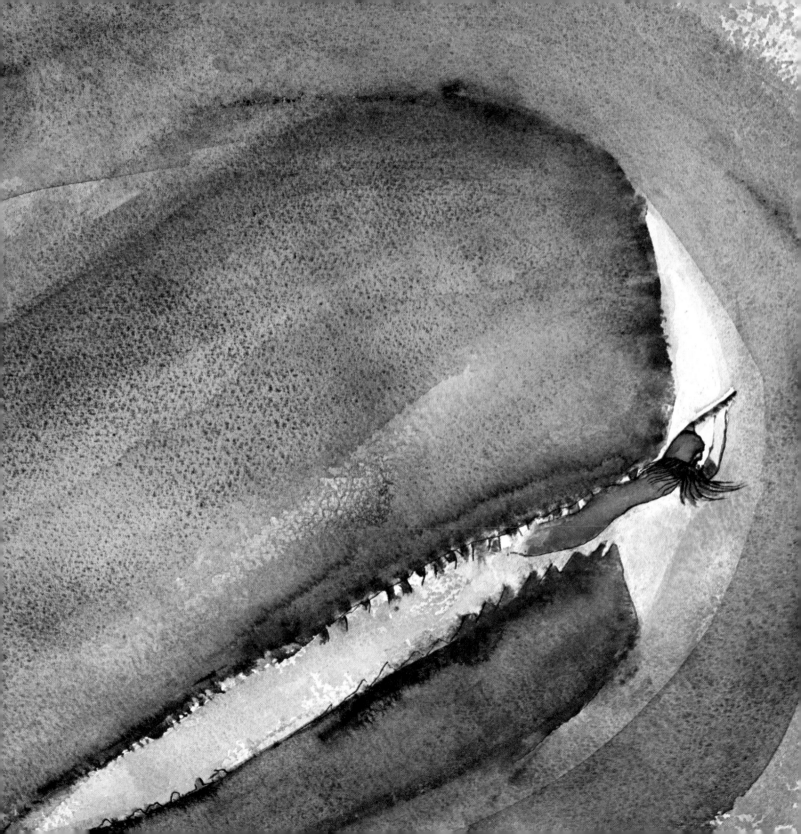

I began my journey to Nineveh
to keep my promise.

I entered the city of the great
winged bulls and began to preach.
"In forty days Nineveh will be
destroyed! God asks only that his
people do justice and love
kindness and walk humbly with
him. But you are a wicked and
violent people. Repent or God will
destroy you."

The people listened
and believed.
The king humbled
himself before the
Lord God and
proclaimed that
all the people of
Nineveh would
put on sackcloth
and ashes to show
God that they
had repented.

Everyone fasted, even the beasts.
And God spared Nineveh.

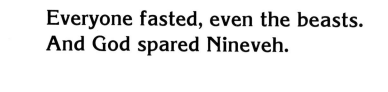

I had prophesied doom,
but Nineveh was saved.
My people would call
me a prophet of lies.
I felt angry. Angry
enough to die.

I climbed a hillside to
brood on my misery.
It was hot and I was
thankful when a vine
sprang up and its
leaves gave me shade.
I was weary with pain
and I fell into a sound
sleep.

While I slept, God commanded a worm to cut down my vine. When I awoke and saw the withered leaves, my anger returned. Why was God mocking me?

God spoke to me then. "Jonah, do you think you have good reason to be angry? You weep for a vine that grew in a night and perished in a night. It was not your vine. You did nothing to make it grow. And now you think I should have spared the vine for your sake. What of Nineveh, Jonah? There are people there who do not know their right hand from their left, and many animals that have done no wrong. These are my children, whom I have nourished and given life. If you pity a vine, should I not pity Nineveh?"

I was ashamed, but I wept for joy.

BEVERLY BRODSKY is a painter with three previous books to her credit. THE CRYSTAL APPLE and SEDNA were published in 1974 and 1975. THE GOLEM: A JEWISH LEGEND was named a 1977 Caldecott Honor Book. She was born in Brooklyn and graduated from Brooklyn College with a bachelor of arts degree. Ms. Brodsky lives in Connecticut, where she paints and writes and illustrates children's books.